ME

WE

Dedicated to:

Myself

You have always been someone who looks for nothing but the good in people and for once you started to see the greatness within yourself. So I dedicate this book to you because growth brought these words forth and God still has many blessings to come. Remember to always stay focus, continue to pray, and never give up on your dreams.

-T.M.

Dedicated to:

My Friends & Family

Thank you for always keeping me inspired and reminding me of how important my voice is. I never take the moments and lessons you share with me for granted. I am grateful to be blessed with each every one of you around me!

-T.M.

Roll Call

1. **Bio**
    - *M.E.*
    - *Vibes*
    - *Hustle*
    - *Dreamer*
    - *The Hero*
2. **Flaws**
    - *Protection*
    - *Pain*
    - *Running*
    - *Invisible*
    - *Help*
3. **Necessities**
    - *Honesty*
    - *Motive*
    - *Communication*
    - *Challenges*
    - *Kisses*
4. **In Between**
    - *Say My Name…*
    - *Snack*
    - *Perception*
    - *The Gray*
    - *Distance*
5. **U.S.**
    - *Empire*
    - *Differences*
    - *Essence*
    - *Quality Time*
    - *W.E.*

Bio

Me

I like ice cream in the
winter time

I prefer music more
than people at times

I'm an introvert and an
extrovert in the same
sentence

I attract people but I
keep my space limited

Thought process
different from most

I have experienced
enough to witness my
growth

Still think the best of
the ones I loved

Sometimes I feel the bar
was too high for their
love

But I still try to be the
love I aspire

Reading books and
watching movies to
stay inspired

Passionate emotions
which lead to trouble

So I picked up a pencil
to remain humble

Writing for a while
now to process my
thoughts

Some of its junk and
others are a work of art

Speaking of art I dabble
in it a little bit

Picasso style and a
little Van Gogh when I
see fit

Now when it comes to
me sharing myself with
other people that is rare

I'm very unique to the
point that people often
stop and stare

As if someone with a
good heart couldn't
possibly exist in this
world

Or that genuine
kindness and love was a
rare mineral hidden
below the earth

In a world full of
corruption, greed, fear,
and pain

I'm the one considered
insane

For not settling or
sticking to the
standards and boxes
that society checked
offed for me

I am my own person
inside and out who are
you to tell me who I
should be

So before you take this
journey to explore my
world

You must first know
that I am not your
typical girl

For words are not
easily accepted

Before there can be a we
you must first learn me
if I'm not mistaken

Vibes

The unspoken truth
between two or more
people

Representing intuition

That you were wishing
wasn't true

Letting you know of

Deception

Collection

Players

& Nonbelievers

Women Lie

Men Lie

But vibes are honest
with you

But you can't doubt the
vibes shown to you

Then get played or
walked on like you
didn't know what was
coming to you

The signs are all
around you from

The things you believe

To the things you
perceive

Everyone wants
something out of life
whether its

Peace

Love

or Wealth

And then there are
some who need a little
help

And that my friend is
where the vibe comes in

It has grown with you
from birth to now

Sometimes you are the
reason for loosening
your own crown

Because you doubted
your intuition

That you get stranded
from the mission

Thats not the goal or
outcome you are trying
to achieve

You must dig deeper to
get the things you want
received

You won't always agree
with the vibe given

But it didn't ask for
your approval nor
permission

The vibe is there to
protect you at all cost

So you can win more
than what you've lost

But you know being the
human beings that we
are

We are so stubborned
causing unforgettable
scars

So let me share
something with you
that you didn't know

The vibe isn't just you
but also the lord who
knows

And the universe too

Trying to save you
heart break and
heartache so you can be
a better you

Everyone accepts trials
and tribulations
differently

Some rush through
others take it gently

Sometimes God calms
the storm, and
sometimes he lets the
storm rage and calms
the child

Figure out which side
you will be on while the
storm goes wild

Trust your instincts
and gut feelings

Its apart of your
natural healing

Vibes will always keep
it true

Remember

Men Lie

Women Lie

But vibes are honest
with you

Hustle

*I get trophies and
awards for my hustle*

*Because I grind
nonstop*

1 job

2 jobs

3 jobs

*Whatever is necessary
to get the job done*

*Now in no way shape
or form am I being
illegal*

*I just work hard to
make myself regal*

*See my ancestors were
Kings and Queens
stripped of their land
and possessions*

*So I'm just reclaiming
what's mine, making
my own corrections*

*I wasn't raised with a
poor man's mentality*

*You go after what you
want regardless of
reality*

Where there's a will
there's a way

And no is not in my
vocabulary

Momma always said
man don't work man
don't eat

So I make sure to stay
on my job but keep my
plans discreet

I work so hard because I
want to be my own
boss

No worries I promise
not to get lost in the
sauce

I want to be able to pay
my mom back tenfold

Because I know raising
me took a lot to mold

But your grace, mercy,
and love kept me whole

And dad well I just
want to make him
proud

See he instilled in me to
not rely on others to
straighten your crown

That sometimes you
have to pick your own
self off the ground

While my little brother
still watches my every
play

Its only right that I
make sure he has a clear
path for his missions to
take place

Hard work over talent
any day is how you
play the cards

I am my brothers keeper
and vice versa for him

He's forever shooting
with me in the gym

So I hustle for

The love of my family

My passion and drive

Always keeping the
Lord by my side

I get awards and
trophies because I
hustle so hard

Dreamer

Constantly on my own
time,
as I watch the pages go
by

With my mind in
constraints
its hard to stay present
in one place

Always getting
criticized because not
many could see,
the things I am
destined to be

A creative high like no
other, if only there was
a group of us to share
our dreams with one
another

A creative space where
creatives breathe freely
Not bound to the
doubts, worries, and
limits man puts in their
route

Would paint the whole
world if I could,

because art in all forms
speaks louder than
words do

If people would listen
more than laugh, a lot
more things would
come to pass

But nonetheless the
time will come,

because for a dreamer
the job is never done

The Hero

Fluent in honor and
grace

Continue to hear
praises from place to
place

Ones for an unspoken
hero

True to their core
values and morals

Roaming the earth as if
they're immortal

You know its bad when
your mom says

"You're such a big hero
to others,

But whose a hero for
you?"

I smiled

It comes with the
territory

Sometimes I have to be
that hero too

Healing wounds
without hesitation

Wouldn't doubt it was
my occupation

Having the ears to
listen to broken words

Fighting those demons
who caused the burns

Helping you regain
strength to defend
yourself

Costing my value and
wealth

One thing about being
a hero is

Someone always needs
saving

But that doesn't
necessarily mean
they're staying

Pick them up and help
them grow

Just to see them leave
you for something more

The only hero there in
their time of struggle

Blinded from the truth
you could not juggle

A hero was never the
need

Only special treatment
for the greed

Always remember to be
a hero to you

Because at the end of
the day a hero needs a
hero too

Flaws

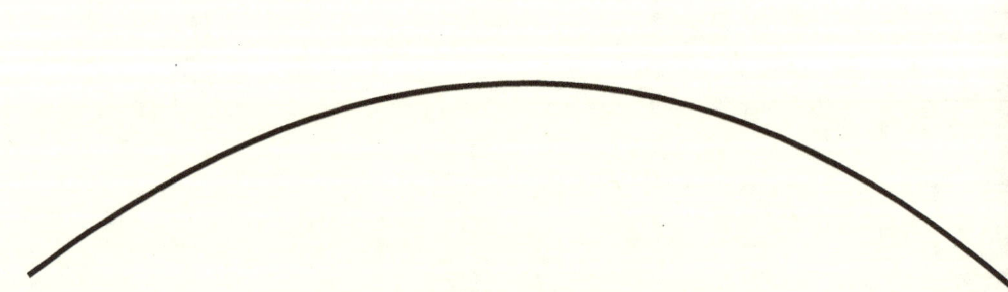

Protection

I get chastised for being
so defensive

I'm sorry its a force of
habit

Not really use to this

To be able to trust
someone else

No I don't have trust
issues

I am just use to doing
things myself

Me,

Myself,

&

I

Those are my body
guards or

My detail squad if you
will

Just being cautious you
see

Not many have been
worthy of me giving
them myself to keep

But my defense system
is a blessing and a
curse

So let's start from the
beginning

Before things turned
for the worse

See I use to get bullied
a lot

For some reason people
had a problem with me

But I on the other hand
was minding my
business listening to
music in peace

And it didn't truly
bother me all that much

Until my retaliation
was seen as the problem
and not the solution

I was accused of crying
wolf

While others just
jumped to conclusions

So I had to get smarter
at how I was protected

I'm the first born so
figuring things out was
like natural selection

I am a scientist so
running experiments
are my expertise

I studied my enemies
playbook like I was
playing in the NBA
Finals with World
Peace

I grew more and more
clever to there antics

Not aware of myself
causing damage

See my defense system got out of hand

Going off script and having their own plans

So use to always being guarded

I low key became cold hearted

Next thing you know I am

Fighting my love ones

Fighting my friends

And even fighting myself

I needed to change my over protective mentality

How am I suppose to grow if I always think people are attacking me

That is not how I want to be seen

Nor the legacy I want to leave behind

So I got better at protecting myself

Striving more to keep my values and morals intact

Being more aware of the things I attract

While keeping an open
mind as new roots lay
tracks

Pain

They say you grow
through the things you
don't have control over

Well what happens
when you feel useless

No bother in trying

No bother in feeling

No bother in living

I heard that pain is in
the mind

But if you read that
from behind

The mind is in pain

See I feel as though
people do not truly
break down that
statement

Because physical pain
and mental pain are not
related

The body physically
heals itself

Mental is going to need
more than just health

The above statement
insist that your pain is
not real it is in the
mind and therefore
nothing but fear in the
perception of pain

Hmmmm……adequate
suggestion

But what happens
when the mind is
hurting

Is the pain still a
figment of my
imagination

A lot of people check on
you by asking how are
you or how are you
doing

I do the same but I also
ask the question how is
your mental

Because I am aware
that tiredness is not
just physical

Draining is not in the
form of bleeding but
still holds the same
effect

And a fever may not
authenticate my
sickness

But I am not well

My mental is tired

I am exhausted from fighting these wars that were before me with no rest in between

My mental cannot always process what is put in front of me

I heal myself I don't have anyone else that I can vent everything to

Just give me some time to think things through

Healing

Is indeed needed for my mental has exhausted its capacity

And this pain cuts deeper than the audacity

You feel to tell me it is unreal

I am mentally strong

For God gives the toughest battles to the strongest warriors

But even the greats need to rest some time

So no everyday won't be bright and everyday won't be blue

But that doesn't mean after this day things won't be new

A new start for a new
day

The healing comes
gradually

For my physical pain
and my mental pain are
not the same

And although the tears
may roll down my face

Just know my mental is
being put back in place

I will not fall victim to
the things that may
cause me pain from
time to time

But I will take the time
to heal what is sacred to
me

Regaining strength for
what is to come

For a warrior the work
is never done

Running

I am a victim

A victim of believing
that time is infinite

And even though I
can't control the things
that happened to me, I
still have to make
decisions in a timely
fashion

I am a victim

A victim of
procrastination

Running from things I
should have resolved a
long time ago

Thinking they would
dissolve on their own

Knowing the questions
that grew hungry for
answers would die out

And the want for
closure would dry out

Running

Known as a code nike
in the public school
system

My laces tied and my
soles firm

For my stride was a
mile long

Reaching for distance
regardless of direction
and strain

Moving with the
extension until I feel no
pain

Running

But not a sprint
necessarily

See there were things I
answered, but
everything else I had to
carry

I didn't have the
answers, let alone knew
what to say

With the baggage
weighing heavy, I
became the best runner
in the game

A victim of my own
misunderstanding

Causing dysfunctional
conclusions as
outcomes where I was
standing

Not wanting to live in
anymore disorder

I tried to gather myself
so I can do what is
right

I started reading
because in order to fix
what was broken

I first needed to
understand what was
never spoken

Why did I view myself
as

the enemy

the fixer

the beginning and the
end

Why were things so
heavy

SPEAK UP

A close mouth doesn't
get fed

And always be aware of
the things you say

I had such a fixation of
how other people felt

That I forgot to look at
myself

As a reminder that
everyone else is a
consideration

I am only expected to
uphold my own
expectations

I am honest, I work
hard to do my best

And I am not always
on the right side of
things

But that doesn't mean
that I am any less of

A woman

A human being

Or myself

And it certainly doesn't
diminish the value of
my wealth

So I hung up my laces
because I no longer

Knew where I was
running to

But at the same time I
wanted to start
something new

A new perspective on
what was
comprehended

Instead of what people
pretended to be true

Running became
obsolete

And honesty was the
ground that was below
my feet

Transparency is what I stood by

While staying true to me was all I seek

I no longer needed others validation

But they did become a demonstration

For what I will no longer accept

I am not ruled by riches but in the pursuit of

Wealth

Happiness

Wisdom

And Prosperity

I am out of the running game to an extent
More focused on being authentic

But I'm grateful for the lessons it taught me

Being true to yourself is worth more than any copy

Invisible

I use to think I was
invisible when I was
younger

Funny I know

More than average
height and I think I am
invisible

I learned at a early age
that people see what
they want to see

So I wasn't truly
invisible just ignored or
overlooked by my peers

And it is true what
they say children are
not born with hate in
their hearts

But rather taught hate
from others later on

I never was one who
wanted to fit in or even
be popular

I have always known
who I was since day
one

But others not so much

They would fault me for their short comings because I was aware of my flaws

And I refuse to let my weaknesses lead to my downfall

So like any great superhero I have read about

I learned to hide in plain sight

Now before the judgement starts to place blame

Allow me to explain

I did what I had to

To survie

See I had to go to school with these kids for middle and high

And high school was better

See by that time I mastered the game no matter the location or weather

But in all seriousness

I learned how to survey my surroundings

See words can mislead

But actions truly show
the story you weren't
told

I am grateful for the
opportunity it has
protected me in the
long run

Being able to
distinguish those who
value words from those
who gave you what you
wanted to hear

This is when it hit me
what mom would
always say

"You have a good heart,
but everyone is not the
same.

And not everyone sees
the good in people like
you do."

She was right

People do what they
want to

See you are not visible
to those who have
nothing to gain from
you

Until you show them
something they like

This could be directly

Indirectly

Or word of mouth

Either way you aren't
noticeable to them until
they see you

But see I am not a fool

And I am very
observant

The same people who
look for you now were
the same ones cracking
jokes about you

And although
forgiveness is always
the greatest practice

Learning from
experiences is a lesson
within itself

Plus I like to live in the
present and not the
past

So just leave those
people where they are at

But the kicker that got
me was when the
invisibility was present
in the relationships as
well you see

I get so amused by the
things I am told

I am aware of my
shortcomings I know
where to grow

But the thing that
amuses me the most

Was when I interact
with someone but often
seem to be a ghost

I am honest and one
hundred percent myself
with the people I date

So I never understood
why they were so late

Late in seeing what I
am capable of

Doubting my skill set
as if it was nonexistent

Intimidated by my
intelligence as if it was
the worse thing to ever
happen

Or me being so
different from the
women you have had in
the past that you
thought I needed
correction

Then I stopped and did
some reflecting

I don't have to accept
any less than what I
deserve

You thought you could
put me in a box, but
that didn't occur

I was outspoken, hard
working, resilient, and
prayed up

You should have just
left me alone if you
didn't have the same
intentions

Same usual women you
are use to controlling

See I am a rare breed
you should have known
better when you were
trolling

I peep everything

Even the things you
least expected

I'm a great listener but
an even better detective

A scientist whose
research skills are
adequate and effective

I am a Melanin Queen
whose value cannot be
dented

Nor broken into pieces
for your contentment

I will not be picked over
for your consumption

Because you found it
difficult to deal with a
real ones construction

I am one of a kind fine
as wine, I get better
with time

My space is limited and
I limit the access to it

Because I want good
vibes and prosperous
vibrations

Not stress and
complications

But the fact of the
matter is the joke is on
you

Because you thought I
was invisible too

Help

I need help

I stretch my hand out
only to find an empty
space

Forever being told to
ask for help because I'd
rather take its position

Being independent not
because I feel superior
to anyone else

But by the time you
count on someone else,
the job would have be
done myself

I need help

The words run through
my mind

Being ignorant to the
man upstairs who
continues to throw
signs

Been let down so much
the experiment tested
negative every time

If my last decision was
you, I rather be doing
the job myself without
a clue

Call it stubborn

Call it protective

Call it bias

Can't help but think
you feel the same way
too

Do you need help?

I was asked or rather I
am asked on a daily

But I stopped my
inquiries, could you
blame me

See people want to help
only in ways that
benefit them

They'll lure you in give
you the tools needed to
complete the task,

Then say the executive
decision was you're
voted out with a slap
on the ass

As if that wasn't any
better reason for them
to rub it in your face,

You feel naive that you
fell for the chase

And hope

Of finally having less
luggage to carry
everyday

That you could breathe
without an oxygen tank
for a couple of hours

That for once all the
pieces to the puzzle
started to reveal a
portrait worth viewing

Help

Shouldn't be shown in
the light this way

It's suppose to be

kind

genuine

authentic

It's suppose to give

relief

serve
hope

and bring joy

I guess that's why I'll
keep believing in it

Although I may not
always be a witness to
what help can do

I will still continue to
help those who do

Necessities

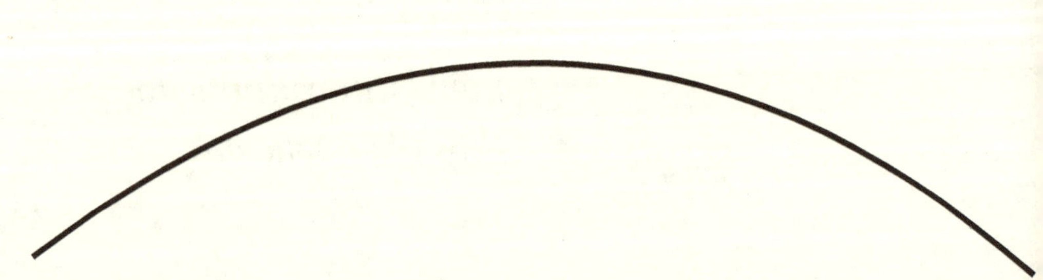

Honesty

When I was younger I
was told

that you should always
tell the truth

Well as time continued

You realize that
honesty

Isn't as profound

But I always knew that
it was the

best ground

Trying to stay true in a
world infested with lies

Always knowing the
truth lies within your
eyes

Appraised for my
strong eye contact

But I wanted to stay far
from the death traps

Because dishonesty
leads to pain

Which lead to tears of
countless rain

With no way out the
light was brought to the
darkness

Yet people still
continued to be so
heartless

Wondering if the lesson
will ever be learned

Of all the lies you have
told

They will come back
increased

As time continues to
turn

Motive

To focused on the
things I want out of

life to be told what I
should do

when my determination
is as strong as gorilla
glue

Often times people
can't see the vision you
have for yourself

But not everything is
meant for everybody

So don't block your
blessings by worrying
about everyone else

My desire is simply
fueled by the things
that I hold close

God, family, and love

Are the reasons for my
gross

Gross as in
development, growth,
and total blessings
earned

Always praying to the
Lord above to show my
gratitude in return

Too motivated to give up on anything

Because the motto is

"Success over Everything"

With the underling being

'Stay true to yourself'

I am aware of my wealth

Too motivated to accept anything less than I deserve

I'm a Melanin Queen I know my worth

All in all

and still till this day

life would be nothing

without peace, love, and family

Always keeping God #1

Knowing he made it all possible

For the blessings to come

Communication

They say
communication is key

Which is true

But do we really know
what it means to
communicate

To communicate

You express your
ideals, passions, and
fears amongst the ones
you trust

This does not mean to
push your ideals,
passions, and
insecurities on someone
who doesn't have the
same lust you do for
your dreams

Words will be exchange
but not to be
inconsiderate

But rather to express
the importance of
separability

Stressing the
significance of
individuality is key

Differences bring you
together to make a
harmonious system

Producing the same product shows no growth, nor junction

To communicate

Is to articulate your feelings, emotions, concerns, and worries in an effective way that the receiver can transmit

The best way to make sure you're heard

Is by saying what you mean,

And meaning what you say

Words that are pure in heart, mind, and soul

Are easier in flow

The recipient is more open minded with an open heart

False words cause mistrust

And lead to confusion and lust

True love is built with honesty and understanding

A clear view with an easy landing

To communicate

Is a passage

From the thoughts that roam my mind when I think of you

To the stress that rattles my insides from time to time

But still I stay on track

En route to your ears

My words flow from the root of my mouth

Chipping the curves of my outer lip

Still keeping my eyes on the distance ahead

The words still move at a steady pace

With the same mission in place

The cue card hanging from my shoulder

As the words brush between your hair

And caress the outer lobe of your ear

Riding the canal to the landing point

You hear............

Nothing

Because you were so
focused on how to
respond

That you couldn't hear
me say

I love you and that I
care

Of all the wonders to
think this all could
have been accomplished

From one simple thing

But you didn't know
what to think,

Because you didn't
know how to
communicate

Challenges

A wise man once told
me the world is hardly
black & white

And he was right

Your first car may not
be ideal

But it's four wheels
that gets you to and
from

Your first love might
not be the first person
you like

But you got to
experience love

And even though they
may not stay

Whose to say that's the
love your suppose to
end up with in the first
place

That college degree may
take you longer than 4
years

But that doesn't make
you any less of a
scholar

Rome wasn't built over night

And bridges burn and doors close

But doors open as well

Challenges were made to make you stronger and to teach perseverance and value in the things you've worked for

They are big and also small

But the deciding factor is you

How will you approach this difficulty?

What is your mindset during the journey?

If the situation persist will you keep going or give up?

Challenges will always be what it is.

A challenge

At the end of the day you make the results.

Kisses

Healing in the form of sweetness

Seductive and luscious

Calming and centered

Once entered in

the mind never lingers

Often at different tempos

depending on the emotion

Crisp and pure

Breathing almost seems uncertain

Holding on

While barely feeling at all

Focused

With no hesitation

Fresh

Sensational

Elegant

Ravishing

Kiss

A sweet creation

In Between

Say My Name..........

I am the war between two people

I am the light in your darkest hour

I keep life a float

But if toyed with I can make you drown with no effort only gloat

I put a smile on your face as my presence wraps around your waist

I am the beginning and the end

I am your drive, your determination, your support, your confrontation

I am the peace between your significant other

I am the joy for your
mother

I am the praise of your
friends

I am a sibling to those
you hold within

I am delicate and whit
and a weapon when fit

I am the ultimatum
you've always had

Never were my
intentions to make you
sad

I am given and taken
away

Never do I come to play

All I want is
understanding, but
most don't know how
to grasp me

I'm spoken too and
rejected often times I
can't even be projected

I'm strong and
powerful needless to
say

But let me introduce
myself the proper way

Hi! My name is
***LOVE**!*

Snack

A snack

Known as something to

Temporarily fill your needs

Until later

See I have a big appetite

I crave knowledge

Thirst for love

And music I can't live without

Well my question to you is

Why have something temporary

Instead of everlasting

A snack is for those who want

Temporary things

Things easily returned back where they came from

Things with expiration dates that don't exceed two weeks

A snack is material vs. sentimental

See,

I need substance

I need long lasting fulfillment

I need support without barriers

I need love without limits

I need laughter without judgment

And happiness with no regrets

So like I said I have a big appetite

Because I am no less than satisfaction

Baby, I'm your greatest caption

That spark that stays ablaze

Through those dark times

You try to hold me captive but

I make my own rules

With my own dime

Because the only standards I'm

Required to meet are
my own

So no I'm not a snack

I'm food to your
soul.

Perception

The things we perceive often wear more than one face

How you see a lake, may not be how your neighbor sees the lake

How you feel a painting, may not feel the same to your best friend

Perception is the key to understanding

For instance ***Jealousy***

I will not get upset if eyes wander towards my lover

I know what I signed up for

Intelligence

Hard Working

Creative

Confident

Pose and Beauty beyond measures

You can't get worked
up over things you put
yourself into

Plus,

Because of the
communication, worth,
and understanding we
have between each
other

Regardless of how
many eyes lay on them

We only have eyes for
one another

Now others would
disagree

"You're not showing
that you'll fight for me,
how will I know the
value I hold with you?"

Perspective is key

Because I know your
worth and how
valuable you are

I am aware of those who
would also like to be in
your space

Perspective is the core
of perception

How you perceive
things will determine
your outcome

Don't let your feel for water colors

Blur your view of the master piece in front of you

When I see you my perception is………

A song without words

Coursing through my veins bringing life to the source of my existence

My eyes are electrified by your beauty

That my muscular system overlooks its purpose

Hypnotized by your work ethic and passion for your dreams

I'm just coasting along side fueling your transit

And once the time has come

Where two become one

Time is diminished and space becomes infinite

So tell me what do you see

When you see me?

What is your
Perception?

The Gray

What is it about the
gray areas that make
people uncomfortable?

Uncomfortable to admit
the flaws they fall
victim to

The love they let get
away because they were
so focused on the future
that they couldn't be
present

Or that just like
everyone else in the
world they make
mistakes and that's
okay

The gray carries your

Fears

Insecurities

Reality

Truths

Facts

Dreams

You become so consumed in how the world wants you to be instead of just being you

There should be more conversations about dreams becoming reality

Because the only person preventing it from becoming true is you

There should be more conversations about fears

So you can stop using them as a handicap to not get things done and try to work through them

There should be more conversations about insecurities

Because they do not justify the way you act towards people or

choose to behave in
general

There should be more
conversations about
truths

Because there is no
need to hide your
truths because others
are too scared to face
their own

There should be more
conversations about
facts

Because anyone can
gossip about garbage
but rarely do you hear
chatter about the things
that matter

So why not challenge
yourself

I want to propose a
toast

To making the
uncomfortable
comfortable

To the gray areas in life

Distance

Let's discuss the spaces
that are placed between
words and how the sky
is between space and
the earth

Or how an hour versus
20 minutes is more
convenient for you than
to discuss the distance
between the two

Right distance

The measurement of
how far apart objects
are

Like you, me, and the
words that should be
between us

Instead there's distance

Distance because fears
over cloud the
possibilities

And you want things
that are easy to come by
instead of building
something worth
lasting

Distance interfering
with our love language
that supersedes the
bond that was created
in the spaces we
vacated to integrate
with each other

I love you

Is distant.....

The bond that extends
from my heart to yours
attacked at the core by

insecurities

deception

lack of communication

uncertainty

Our bond tainted by
distance

This is the time we rely
on the trust, faith, and
love within one another

But the distance blew
our cover

Seeping through the
cracks filling areas
where roots once laid

Look me in the eyes and
say it

I love you

And that no distance
between us could ever
replace the tracks we
have laid to find our
place

I apologize for you felt I
wasn't here with you in
time

But you left me in this
realm to defend for
myself that I couldn't
feel your presence next
to mine

I am thinking we while
you are busy thinking
me and moving on your
own while I was still
moving for us you see

You had the audacity to
say I just wanted you
for lust

So listen while I speak
because I am only
going to say this once

Distance grew between
us in place with your
doubts, worries, and
facade you grew
accustom to because

I am not one to leave
you alone nor forsake
you

I plan accordingly
when it comes to love
and I didn't want to
rush

But you grew
impatient and stopped
looking at my love

So don't tell me I'm the
enemy who longed for
lust, making love to
you was far beyond
anything you could
combust

And I will no longer
continue to feel sorry
for the monster you
have created

Instead of remembering
the lover you
domesticated

I can't continue to
bandage wounds I
didn't create then take a
knife to the heart like a
prime rib steak

I am one person

And one person only

Trying to make it in
this world without
anymore distance
created by my hands

Tired of being in a room
full of people that I
know head to toe

But disconnected
because of incidents
that caused distantness

So no we could have
worked

We would have worked

But your quickness

Resulted in my
constant stress

About situations we
could never address

Leaving me to battle for
myself

While you worked on
your wealth

But I was determined

It was my mission

To get back to the love
we created one step at a
time

Knowing how much I
believed in the things
we aligned

Mentally, physically,
emotionally building

Steady while I was
loosing feeling

Battling distance
because I don't believe
in its existence

Fighting for you felt
unrealistic

One day the distance
won't be visible to the
eye

And by then the only
thing left to face is you
and I

U.S.

Empire

Two people building
together outside of
standard outcomes

Refusing to give up on
each other

Steady preparing one
another

Communicating in
ways comprehension is
spoken

Collecting all the
rewards that were owed

Pushing one another to
be the best they can be

Like Barack Obama and
Michelle

Whats a King without
a Queen

Pulling a Beyonce and
Jay-Z we are on the run
for all that is ours

Reclaiming our time for
every mile of every
hour

Staying true to the
three values we hold
close

God, family, and love

Will keep us on the go

While blessings rain
from above

Knowing the ride won't
be smooth

We will continue to
focus on the love

But look me in the eyes
and tell me that its true

That we are going to
take over the world just
me and you

No I'm not discussing
in ways of power that's
real

It grows in the epitome
of evil and I don't want
that deal

I am talking about
peace in knowing that
we don't have to stress
about who is doing
what

Because everything is
already said and done

I am discussing the
worth knowing that I
got your back and you
have mines

And like Michelle
stated I don't need any
weak players on my
team

So don't waste my time

The fact that no stranger, past life lover, friend, or family member could intersect what we have built

Doubt

Fear

Insecurities

Become revealed

They won't be able to fester in this world that was created with our hands

And you won't hesitate to fight back

To restore order and balance to the land

Because this empire we are building will take determination and patience

Nothing less of hard work and dedication

And success won't come easy

But its worth it believe me

Because anything worth having is worth working for

So if you feel this is too much for you then
Go there is the door

Be honest with me because

Honesty kills assumptions

I want answers from the source

Not those who make up thoughts from corruption

And if you can't stay focus on the mission at state

Then its only right you cancel those remaining dates

And if you seek to have what others have because you feel as though you deserve it

You have no idea what soul they had to sell to earn it

And even if they didn't

Jealousy is still a sickness

Which leads me to my last topic but the most important of them all

Are you religious, spiritual, or nothing at all

Because I praise my savior for life and blessings

I pray when things are great or messy

But most of all the source for everything

So I need faith, hope, love, and support by my side

Wakanda forever is the motto I stand by

There is no need to get upset for me asking the important questions

We are both grown adults trying for out best interests

So what have you concurred from this interesting conversation

Are you ready to build this empire

Or are you still contemplating?

Differences

I am fire and you are
water

You are day, I am night

And with all these
differences

Things still worked out
just right

You were dark and I
was your light

I was anxious and your
were gentle

Never letting me get
lost in my mental

You were my sanity, I
am your peace

Both praying to the
Lord above

To watch each others
feet

For where we stepped
was not always
together

Neither one was too far
in the stormy weather

Nonetheless we always
found our way

Refusing to let the
other stray

But our differences had
us make inferences
About what this could
have been

But we let our
differences test the
time, Leaving all the
drama behind

Our uniqueness is
what makes our
interests become in
sync with each other

Working in unison as if
we were the perfect
pieces to the puzzle

Its when our differences
align

That we rarely seem
different at all

Like perfect symmetry

You will always be the
one I can call home

The salt to my pepper

Because the seasoning
is just right

The milk to my honey

Because we flow so
easily by each others
side

The Mary Jane to my
Rick James

Because a puff of you
makes the pain go away

The Jada to my Will

Because you allow
silliness to be fulfilled

The storm to my black
panther

Because their bond was
infinite

No matter the distance
or struggles that
crossed their paths

They always stayed
true to what they had

So glad our differences
could explain it to me

Because there is no
other place

I would rather be

Than enjoying the
differences that made
love between you and
me

Essence

I want to get lost in
your essence

See my body feeds off of
our connection

Giving my heart an
injection

That couldn't be
detected

Because your soul cries
out to me for affection

Your supernatural aura

Compels me to think
you are an angel in
human form

But then again I start
to brainstorm

No not an angel but a
miracle unseen

"What, what does that
mean?"

See miracles are
miraculous, unseen
possibilities,

Events, happiness that
strucks you from afar

Meaning your view
upon my eyes makes me

feel as though I fell for a star

An unseen miracle causing a rhythmic error in my heart as it flows

How I continued to stand there no one knows

I want to feel your essence

Because only you could explain the complexion

Down to every detail and section

They say we attract our reflections

So if you are my imperfections

Then I love you without exceptions

Because only my reflection would reveal what is deep inside

Being with you helps me enjoy the ride

I want to be immersed in your essence

Because only the Lord knows the feeling you leave in my presence

And if time could be endless

I would render this
moment with you
relentless

You are the drug that
fuels my addiction

But also frees me of
conviction

And if tomorrow never
existed

I would still know what
this is

Because your love is
my jurisdiction, that
frees me of conviction,
but also my addiction,

and I refuse to make
predictions

Because the future
doesn't flourish
without work in the
present

Baby I want to get lost
in your essence

Quality Time

Fresh air kissing my
cheeks

Deep breathe of time
roaming free

Routing my eyes to seal
with yours

Your hand follows with
its own melody and
chords

Floating free in this
existing space

Creating a time zone
with no location to
trace

Shut out from the
outside world

My focus staying true
to those two words

Quality Time

Listening to the
vibrations of one
another's auras

Decoding the hidden
language of two lovers

Time with no hands

Spontaneous yet
something planned

Exploration with the
words unsaid

Crucial to the journey
ahead

Understanding the
peak at its core

Significant to the
things in store

Quality Time

Healing each others
battle scars

Preparing for the
journey back is so hard

Your new favorite place
will test the time

Yearning for what is
known as

Quality Time

We

I don't expect things to be perfect

But I do expect you to be assertive

In your wants, needs, and desire

So we can continue to teach and learn from each other without an

Expire

Deadline

Or cut of date

I know you expect me to relate

But I can only touch as far as your reach can make

We are one

I'm a part of you just as you are a part of me

I need you to promise me something

We keep this thing running

No quitting

No allegations

No dishonesty

Or disloyalty

I'm not matching your energy I'm keeping mines stable because I want to attract what's for me

But your effort

Your determination

Your love

Are a reflection of my own

I won't know everything but you're not searching for the answers alone

And although the weather will not always be transparent

You will not whether the storm alone for I am here with you

Side by side

Ride or die

We meet each other in the middle

We both believe things should be shared equally

You've meet my transgressions, my flaws, my love, and my peace

Since you've met ***ME****, do you still believe in* ***WE****?*

In all aspects of life
always remain
humble to yourself.

~T.M.

www.ingramcontent.com/pod-product-compliance
Lightning Source LLC
LaVergne TN
LVHW051016080826
845145LV00009B/2650